Suddenly the three men came wide awake. Soldiers were coming toward them, their armor clanking.

"Soldiers!" John exclaimed.

"Oh, no!" Peter groaned. For there, in front of the crowd, was Judas Iscariot leading the way.

The mob of soldiers rushed toward Jesus, swords and clubs ready in their hands. Calmly He walked toward them instead of trying to run away as they expected Him to.

"Master!" Judas Iscariot exclaimed, stepping forward to kiss Jesus on the cheek. Then he stepped back. His job was finished.

The soldiers grabbed Jesus. Shouting and waving their swords, they dragged Him away to the house of Caiaphas, the high priest. The chief priests and scribes were waiting there to find a way to have Jesus put to death.

THE KING WHO LIVES FOREVER

Alice Schrage

Regal Books

A Division of G/L Publications
Ventura, CA U.S.A.

Other good reading in this series:
Elijah and Elisha by Ethel Barrett
Joshua by Ethel Barrett
Joseph by Ethel Barrett
Daniel by Ethel Barrett
Ruth by Ethel Barrett
Birth of a King by Alice Schrage

The foreign language publishing of all Regal books is under the direction of GLINT. GLINT provides financial and technical help for the adaptation, translation and publishing of books in more than 85 languages, for millions of people worldwide.

For more information write: GLINT, P.O. Box 6688, Ventura, California 93006.

Scripture quotations in this publication are primarily paraphrased.

Published by Regal Books
A Division of GL Publications
Ventura, California 93006
Printed in U.S.A.

Library of Congress Catalog Card No. 81-50590
ISBN 0-8307-0766-2
RL: 5,6

| Abraham | Joseph | Moses | Joshua | Ruth | Saul | David | Solomon | Elijah | Elisha |
| 1900 | 1290 | | 1000 | | 925 | | 722 | | |

Exodus   Division of Kingdom

Contents

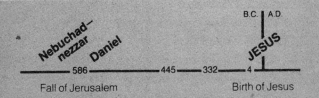

B.C. | A.D.

Nebuchad- nezzar Daniel

JESUS

——586——————445——332——4——

Fall of Jerusalem   Birth of Jesus

1

THE BLIND MAN
John 9:1-38

On a bright Sabbath* morning Jesus walked with His twelve disciples** along a Jerusalem street toward the Temple. They lifted their faces to the bright sunshine which warmed the cool morning air.

Ahead of them a blind man shuffled along, his hand on the shoulder of a small boy. The man was hunched into his ragged coat, and his face was sad. He didn't see the bright sun or notice the freshness of the air.

The disciples watched as the boy led the man to a place near the gate of the Temple. The man slumped down on the ground, his back against the wall.

* The seventh day of the week, a day of rest.
** Men Jesus chose to learn about Him and do a special job.

"Now, Joel, you behave today," the blind man told the boy. "No more chasing chickens or teasing little children."

"Yes, Uncle Simon,"* the boy said. Then he darted away.

"Help the blind," the man began to call out in a sing-song voice. "Help the blind for the love of God."

Jesus and the disciples walked past the blind man toward the gate of the Temple. John, one of the disciples, turned to Jesus. "Why is that man blind?" he asked.

"Maybe he has done some terrible sin that he's being punished for," Philip said. "Or was it his parents who sinned?"

"He isn't being punished for anyone's sin," Jesus answered. "But God wants to show what He can do through this man."

"Help the blind," Simon begged, hearing the voices nearby. He held up his bowl, hoping the disciples would give him a few coins.

*The Bible doesn't tell us the blind man's real name. We'll call him Simon.

Jesus walked over and knelt in front of the man. "I'm Jesus," He said, touching Simon lightly on the arm. Then Jesus spit* on the ground at the man's feet and mixed the saliva with dirt to make mud. Jesus picked up some of the mud between His fingers and patted it on Simon's eyes.

"Now you go," Jesus said, "and wash your eyes in Siloam Pool."

The man sat still for a moment, his face full of questions. Then he got up and took a few careful steps. "Joel!" he called. "Joel, come here!" But the boy was not around.

Simon shuffled along uncertainly. He lifted his face to feel the direction of the sun. Then he headed off slowly, feeling his way toward the city gate.

"I hope he can find Siloam Pool," John said anxiously, looking at Jesus. But Jesus did not answer.

Several hours later Simon returned to Jerusalem. He walked along the street, looking

---

* A common thing to do in the country where Jesus lived, but considered bad manners today.

at everything through wide eyes. He went to
the little room where he lived and looked at his
sleeping mat on the floor and the low table
where he sat to eat his meals. Then he returned
to the street.

"Look!" a neighbor said. "Isn't that Simon,
the blind man?"

"I think it is!" another neighbor exclaimed.

"Sure looks like Simon," said another.
"But it must be someone else. That man is
walking tall and sure, not hunched up like
Simon."

Simon looked around at his neighbors. He
knew all their voices, and now he could see
their faces too. "It's me!" he exclaimed.
"Simon!"

"What happened?" his neighbors asked in
amazement. "Why can you see now?"

"A man named Jesus made some mud and
put it on my eyes," Simon answered. "He told
me to go and wash in Siloam Pool. So I did.
And now I can see!"

"Where is Jesus?" one of the neighbors
asked.

"I don't know," Simon shrugged. He walked off toward the Temple, and some of the neighbors trailed after him.

Outside the Temple, Simon looked at the place where he had sat begging every day. Then he walked into the Temple court with his neighbors following.

"Here," one of the neighbors said, "let's tell the Pharisees* what happened to you." And he led Simon to a group of Pharisees who sat in the corner of the court.

"Remember this man?" the neighbor asked. "The blind beggar at the gate? Now he can see!"

The Pharisees turned to look at Simon. "Yes, I remember you," one of them said. "How did you get your sight?"

"Jesus put mud on my eyes," Simon answered. "And I washed them and now I can see."

"Jesus!" one of the Pharisees hissed. "Today? On the Sabbath?"

* Men who strictly obeyed the Jewish law. They were religious leaders.

Simon nodded.

"Jesus knows the Jewish law says He must not work on the Sabbath," another Pharisee said. "He is not from God."

"But how can a sinner do miracles?" asked another. And soon they were all arguing hotly among themselves about Jesus.

"What do *you* say about Jesus?" one of them finally asked, turning to Simon.

"He must be a prophet," Simon said.

"I think this is a trick," one of the Pharisees said. "The man probably never was blind. Let's call his parents in and check out his story."

The next morning Simon's parents went with him to the Temple. They had heard that the Jewish leaders said anyone who believed in Jesus could not worship in the Temple, and they were very fearful.

"Is this your son?" the leaders asked the old couple.

"Yes." the father answered. "He's our son."

"Was he born blind?"

"He was born blind," said the mother.

"Then how do you explain that he can now see?"

The parents looked at Simon then back at the leaders. "This is our son, and he was born blind. But we do not know why he can now see," the father answered. "Ask him. He's a grown man."

As soon as the leaders would let them, the parents hurried out of the Temple. They didn't stop until they reached home.

The leaders talked together about what the parents said. Then for a second time they called in Simon.

"Listen," they said, "we've decided you should just give praise to God for your sight. We know this man Jesus is a bad man. You needn't mention Him anymore."

"I don't know about His being bad," Simon said. "I just know that I was blind, but now I can see."

"Now, what was it Jesus did to you?" one of the leaders asked. "Tell us again how He gave you your sight."

"I already told you," Simon answered.

"Weren't you listening? Why should I tell it
again?" He looked around at the circle of
angry-faced men. "Do you want to become
Jesus' disciples?" he teased.

"YOU are His disciple!" they exploded.
"We follow Moses. But we don't know where
this Jesus comes from."

"That's interesting," Simon said, feeling
bolder by the second. "You don't know where
Jesus comes from, but He healed my eyes.
You said yourselves that God doesn't listen to
sinners but He hears those who obey Him. No
one before ever gave sight to someone born
blind. If Jesus weren't from God, He couldn't
have done it either!"

"Why, you   you SINNER!" they raged.
"You think you can teach us?" They grabbed
him roughly and pushed him toward the door.
"You're not one of us," they screamed,
pushing him out into the street.

Simon walked slowly home. He felt lonely.
But he also felt peaceful.

The next morning Simon went back to the
Temple. He stood outside, thinking about the

things that had happened since Jesus made his blind eyes to see. Then he felt that someone stood near him. He turned to see Jesus looking at him kindly.

"I hear they threw you out of the Temple yesterday," Jesus said. Then He looked very seriously into Simon's eyes. "Do you believe in the Son of God?" He asked.

"Who is He?" Simon asked breathlessly. "I want to believe in Him."

"You have seen Him," Jesus said. "You are speaking with Him now."

Simon looked at Jesus, and he knew it was true.

"Lord, I believe," he said. And he knelt down at Jesus' feet.

2

WHO IS JESUS?
Luke 9:18-36; Matthew 16:13-20

Jesus sat up and looked around. He had been talking with God, and now He was ready to go on about His work. He looked over at His disciples waiting nearby and smiled.

The disciples always got tired while Jesus prayed. As usual, some of them had fallen asleep. Others talked quietly together. John lay on his back on the ground, looking up at the sky.

Jesus stood up and stretched. Then He walked over to sit down with the disciples.

"What do you hear people saying about me?" He asked them. "Who do they think I am?"

John rolled over on his side, propped his

head on his hand and said, "Some think you're John the Baptist come back to life."

"Or Elijah or Jeremiah,"* Andrew added.

"Or any of the prophets** come back to life."

"And what about you?" Jesus asked, looking around at them. "Who do *you* think I am?"

"You're the Messiah,"*** Peter said firmly, "the Son of God."

Jesus put His hand on Peter's arm. "God has blessed you, Simon**** son of John!" Jesus exclaimed. "No human person told you that. My Father Himself told you."

Then Jesus turned to the other men. "Don't tell anyone that I am the Son of God," He said. "Remember. You must keep this to yourselves."

A few days later Jesus went into the mountains to spend some time praying. He

---

* Two important Old Testament prophets.
** People who received messages from God and told them to other people.
*** Christ the Saviour for whom the Jewish people had waited so long.
**** Peter's official name.

took Peter, James and John with Him and they walked for a long time.

"This is a good place," Jesus finally said, stopping. He went a few feet further on and sat down on the dry, brown earth.

The three men looked around. They could see the valley below and the brown hills they had just climbed. They sat down on the ground and began to pray silently. Later they talked together. Finally they fell asleep. The hours went by so slowly.

In a very special time, Jesus talked with His Father, God. As He prayed, His face began to glow. His clothing became shining white. The brightness seemed to fill the mountainside.

The disciples stirred. They could sense the brightness even before they opened their eyes. Finally they looked up sleepily.

Jesus stood before them in all His shining brightness. Moses and Elijah* had come to stand with Him, and they talked together about the work Jesus still had to do on earth.

* Two important Old Testament prophets.

Suddenly the disciples were wide awake. They had never seen anything like this, and they were frightened.

Then a bright cloud surrounded all of them, and the three disciples huddled together in fear.

"This is my Son whom I love dearly," spoke a voice from the cloud. "I'm very happy with Him. Listen to Him!"

The disciples fell down, their faces on the ground. They were feeling more frightened by the minute.

Then suddenly all was silent. Peter, James and John looked up to see Jesus standing alone. He looked the same as always. All the whiteness and light were gone.

Jesus walked over to the three men. He touched each of them gently on the head.

"Get up," He said. "Don't be afraid."

The men got up and followed Jesus down the mountainside. They walked along in silence, their minds full of what had just happened. Finally Jesus spoke to them.

"Don't tell anyone what you have seen,"

He said. "Don't say a word until the Son of man* rises from the dead."

They nodded. They could never explain what they had seen. It was almost like a dream. Would anyone believe them if they did tell?

But what did Jesus say? "Don't tell anyone until the Son of man rises from the dead."

What could Jesus mean? Somehow they knew He was talking about Himself. The words made them feel sad.

Something very terrible was going to happen to Jesus.

* A name Jesus sometimes called Himself.

3

TWO WHO SERVED OTHERS
Luke 10:25-42

"Teacher!" a man called.

Jesus turned to see a scribe* standing among the people who had gathered to listen to Him teach.

"Teacher," the scribe asked, "what must I do to live forever?" He waited for Jesus' answer with a satisfied look on his face. *I obey all the law,* he thought. *What more could I do?*

Jesus smiled at the satisfied look on the man's face. "What does the law say?" He asked. "How do you read it?"

The scribe looked surprised, but only for

---

* A man who copied the Scripture by hand and was thought to know lots about Jewish law.

an instant. "The law says," he answered,
" 'Love the Lord your God with all your heart,
with all your soul, and with all your strength
and with all your mind,' and 'Love your
neighbor as yourself.' "

"That's right," Jesus said. "If you do that
you will have eternal life."

The scribe didn't like Jesus' answer
because he thought right away of some people
he hated. How could he possibly love
everyone!

"How do I know who my neighbor is?" the
scribe asked.

"Let me tell you a story," Jesus answered.
"A man from Jerusalem traveled to Jericho.
Along the way some thieves waited among the
rocks, watching the road. When the man came
near, they jumped out and surrounded him.

"The man tried to get away, but the thieves
beat him until he fell silent to the ground.
Then they took his clothes and all his money.
They left him half dead and ran back into the
hills to their hiding place.

"The wounded man lay by the road for

many hours. He couldn't move. His whole body hurt.

"Finally a priest* from Jerusalem came riding along. He saw the man lying at the edge of the road.

" 'Those horrible thieves!' he muttered. 'Something has got to be done about them!' And he rode his donkey past on the far side of the road.

"A little later a Levite** came along. 'Ooooh,' he said when he saw the man lying beside the road. The sight of all that blood made him feel sick to his stomach. He slapped his donkey into a trot and hurried by, staying as far away from the wounded man as he could.

"Then along came a Samaritan,***

" 'Oh!' he breathed, pulling his donkey to a stop. He looked quickly up at the hills above the road, but there was no sign of the thieves.

---

* A Jewish man who offered sacrifices and prayers to God for the people.
** A person from the tribe of Levi. Some Levites were priests.
*** A person from a mixed race. Samaritans and Jews usually hated one another.

" 'You poor man,' he said softly, kneeling beside the wounded man. Gently he examined the wounds. Then he took some wine and oil from his supplies on the donkey's back. He cleaned the wounds with wine and poured on oil to soothe them. Then he pulled an extra tunic* from his bag and tore it into strips to bandage the wounds.

" 'No broken bones, thank God,' he said. 'Come, we must get you on the donkey and take you to an inn.'

"The wounded man groaned with pain as the Samaritan helped him get up on the donkey.

" 'I'll take you to Jericho,' the Samaritan said. And he led the donkey with one hand, steadying the wounded man with the other. They traveled very slowly.

"When they arrived in Jericho, the Samaritan found an inn. He arranged a bed in a quiet corner for the wounded man and stayed right beside him all night.

---

* A shirt which slips over the head and comes to the knees or below.

"In the morning he handed some money to the innkeeper. 'Take care of this man,' he said, 'until he can travel. I'll return in a little while, and I'll repay whatever you spend on him.'

"Now," Jesus said, turning to the scribe, "which of the three who passed by on the road to Jericho was a neighbor to the wounded man?"

The scribe was silent for a moment. He didn't want to answer. He didn't like Samaritans. But he finally had to say it. "The one who cared for the wounded man."

"You're right," Jesus said. "Now go and serve people like the Samaritan did."

The scribe no longer felt so sure of his own goodness. Loving his neighbor as much as he loved himself was harder than he had imagined. He walked away slowly, thinking hard about Jesus' story.

Soon Jesus and His disciples walked away also. They traveled to Bethany.

In Bethany a woman named Martha lived with her sister Mary and her brother Lazarus. They liked to have Jesus visit them.

So when they heard that Jesus was coming to Bethany, Martha ran out to meet Him.

"Please come and have supper at our house tonight," Martha said.

"Thank you," Jesus smiled. And when He had finished teaching, He went with His disciples to Martha's house.

Martha had planned a big, delicious supper, and she was very busy preparing the food. She stopped to welcome her guests and to be sure they were comfortable. Then she left them sitting on mats on the floor, talking with her brother Lazarus, and went back to take care of the food.

Mary was helping Martha with the food, but she had a hard time paying attention to her work. She kept stopping to listen to Jesus. Finally she walked over and sat down on the edge of a mat near Him.

Martha frowned at her sister's back. She turned the meat which sizzled on the spit over the fire. Wiping the sweat from her face, she hurried on to mix some rolls.

A few minutes later Mary was still sitting

on the mat listening to Jesus.

"Mary!" Martha called. "Come here!"

But Mary was listening so hard to what Jesus said that she paid no attention to her sister's angry voice.

Finally Martha walked over to stand near Mary. "Mary," she said, "there's so much to do. You have no right to leave me alone with all the work."

Then she turned to Jesus. "Don't you even care, Lord, that my sister sits here while I do all the work? Tell her to help me!"

Jesus smiled at Martha. "You are working hard, Martha," He said, "taking care of us. And you have many things on your mind!"

Martha nodded. It was about time someone noticed how hard she worked!

But Jesus went on. "You could do things more simply," He said. "As for Mary, she has chosen a good part. I will not take it from her."

Martha went back to work, shaking her head. She worked more slowly, for she wanted to think about what Jesus had said. When the food was ready, she served it to her hungry guests.

After everyone had eaten all they wanted, Martha cleared the leftovers away. Then she turned her back on all the dirty dishes and the pots and went to sit on the mat near Jesus.

In the morning, when Jesus was gone, there would be plenty of time to wash the dishes.

4

LOVE OR LAW?
Luke 11:1-13,37-54; 13:10-17

John sat up and rubbed his eyes. He had fallen asleep again while Jesus prayed. "Oh, Jesus," he said, "it's so hard for us to pray with you. We don't know how to pray."

"Lord," Andrew said, sitting up, "teach us to pray."

"Yes," Peter added eagerly. "John taught his disciples to pray. Please teach us."

Jesus sat down with the men. He was silent for a moment, and then He said, "You can pray like this:

Father in heaven,
Holy is your name!
Be the King on earth
  just as you are in heaven.
Give us food every day.
Forgive our sins as we forgive
  those who wrong us.
Don't lead us into temptation,
  but keep us from sin."

Jesus stopped for a moment, and then He
went on. "You must also learn to keep praying
until God answers your prayer.

"Suppose a friend comes to your house late
at night. He has traveled a long way. You
didn't know he was coming, so you have no
food in the house. At midnight you go to your
neighbor and ask for some bread.

"At the neighbor's house, everyone is
sleeping. But you bang on his door until he
asks what you want.

" 'A friend of mine just arrived,' you call,
'and I have no food in the house. Please lend
me some bread so I can give him something to
eat.'

" 'Go home!' the neighbor calls back. 'We are all in bed, I can't give you anything right now!'

" 'But do you have any bread?' you ask. 'I really must have some bread for my friend.'

"If the neighbor won't give you the bread because he's a friend," Jesus went on, "he will surely get up and give you bread just because you keep asking.

"In the same way, when you pray, keep asking God for what you need until He gives it to you.

"Some of you men are fathers," Jesus went on. "When your son asks for a piece of bread, you don't give him a stone instead. Or if he asks for fish, you wouldn't give him a snake."

Peter smiled, thinking about his children at home. Some of the other men murmured their agreement.

"Even more," Jesus added, "my Father in heaven won't give you bad things instead of the gifts you ask of Him. My Father loves you."

"Thank you, Jesus," John said. "Now I

understand better about prayer."

"Come," Jesus said, standing up. "We must go back to the village."

In the village a crowd soon gathered around Jesus. He taught them until evening, and healed the sick people they brought to Him. One day followed another as Jesus and His disciples traveled from village to village.

One evening when Jesus had finished teaching, a Pharisee came to Him.

"Rabbi,"* the Pharisee said, "I would be honored to have you eat with me tonight."

"Thank you," Jesus replied, and He followed the Pharisee home.

Many other Pharisees and scribes soon began arriving at the house. The Pharisee greeted each one of them with a kiss on the cheek, and then a servant washed their feet.** Finally, when the guests were ready to go into the dining room, they washed their hands carefully according to the strict Jewish rules.

Jesus, watching silently, thought about how

* Teacher. A title often used for Jesus.
** The proper way to welcome a guest in those days.

careful they were to obey the law. Yet, they didn't obey God by loving God or their neighbors.

Jesus turned and walked firmly into the dining room without washing His hands. He lay down on one of the divans* around the big table.

The host looked at Jesus, surprised. "You didn't wash your hands, Rabbi," he said.

Jesus sat up and looked around the table. "You Pharisees," He said, speaking to all of them, "make so much of being clean. But your hearts are full of dirt and sin."

The guests gasped. Jesus looked at them sternly.

"You're so concerned about every little detail of the law," He went on. "You make sure to give a tenth of every little herb you plant in your garden. You want the most important seats in the synagogues and like having people bow to you in the market. You think you are so important."

*A bed-like sofa on which people lay with their heads close to the table.

"Teacher," one of the scribes interrupted, sitting up, "when you talk like that to the Pharisees, you're speaking against us scribes, too."

"I certainly am," Jesus agreed. "You scribes consider yourselves experts in the law. But what you say the law means is so difficult for people to do that they have no hope of obeying the law."

Jesus talked on. Finally some of the men jumped up and began to shout at Him.

"You sinner!" they cried angrily. "You don't even know anything about the law!"

Soon after that Jesus left. Then the Pharisees and scribes talked for a long time about how much they hated Him. "We'll catch Him," they said to one another.

"Yes, someday He'll fall into our trap!"

Some time later, when Jesus was teaching in a synagogue, He showed by His actions what He had been trying to tell the Pharisees and scribes.

It was the Sabbath. Jesus had just read the Scripture from the big scroll and handed it back to the leader of the synagogue. He was about to sit down and begin teaching when He noticed a woman coming in the door at the back of the synagogue.

The woman walked very slowly. Each step caused her pain. Her back was so bent that she could not look straight ahead. Jesus knew at once that she had been that way for a long time. He wanted her to be well and strong and straight.

"Lady!" Jesus called.

The woman stopped and tried to look up.

"Lady, you are healed," Jesus said. Then He walked quickly to the back of the synagogue. The men, sitting on mats on the floor, turned to watch Him. Women leaned forward to see what would happen.

When Jesus reached the woman, He put His hands firmly on her shoulders. "You are healed," He said again.

At that very moment, the woman straightened up. She stood tall, her face full of wonder. "Oh, thank you, Lord!" she cried. "Thank you!"

The woman's husband stood nearby, staring at her as if he couldn't believe what had happened. Some of the women rushed over to hug her, exclaiming with joy.

"Silence!" the leader of the synagogue cried, walking through the crowd to the front. "Silence!"

The people quieted down.

"This is wrong!" the leader shouted, glaring at Jesus. Then the leader turned to the people. "There are six days to work. Come and be healed then, not on the Sabbath." He looked angrily at the woman who had just been healed.

Jesus walked quickly to the front of the room. "You pretender!" He exclaimed, looking at the leader. "You will take your ox and your donkey from the barn and lead them to water on the Sabbath. You take care of the animals' needs. This woman has been sick these eighteen years. Isn't it right that she should be healed on the Sabbath? That was her need."

The leader looked down at his feet. *I guess that's right,* he thought.

The people again turned to the woman who had been healed. They were so happy to see her well and strong. Soon the synagogue was filled with the sounds of their praise to God.

5

A STRANGE DINNER PARTY
Luke 14:1-24

Jesus lay on a divan at the big dinner table. He looked around at all the guests. They were rich, important people. Then He looked at His host, Nathan* a leader of the Pharisees.

"Nathan," Jesus said, and the Pharisee turned toward Him. "Nathan, when you have a big dinner, don't invite your friends, brothers and rich neighbors."

Everyone around the table stopped talking and turned to listen to Jesus.

"Why not?" Nathan asked. "Who else would I invite?"

* The Bible doesn't tell us the Pharisee's name, so we'll call him Nathan.

"All of these people will invite you to their homes for dinner," Jesus said, motioning around the table. "They will invite you to repay you for this dinner."

"What's wrong with that?" Nathan asked. Then he added quickly, "No one needs to invite me to their house just because I invited them to my house."

"When you plan a feast," Jesus went on, "invite the poor who never have enough food to eat. Invite the crippled and blind who beg in the streets. They can't pay you back with a dinner. But you'll be rewarded in heaven."

"Oh, it will be wonderful to eat together in heaven!" one of the guests exclaimed.

Jesus turned to the man who had just spoken. "Let me tell you a story," He said. Everyone settled down comfortably to listen.

Jesus told about a man who planned a big party. He made out a list of friends and important people he wanted to invite.

"Oh, thank you! We'll come to the party!" they all promised when they received the invitation.

Then the man began to get ready for the party. He cleaned his house until it sparkled. He prepared the best food he could buy. Finally he set the big table in his dining room.

"Everything is ready," he said to his servant. "Go and tell the guests it's time for the party."

The servant smiled happily as he went to call the guests. But his smile soon disappeared.

"I just bought some land," the first guest told the servant. "I must go and have a look at it right away. Please ask your master to excuse me."

"I bought five pairs of oxen to work in my fields," the second man said. "I was just now leaving to go and try them out. Tell your master I'm sorry."

"I just got married," one said happily. "I can't leave my bride for a party."

The servant went on, speaking to each person his master had invited. Not one of them kept his promise to attend the party. Everyone had some excuse.

Finally the servant went home. "No one

wants to come," he said sadly to his master.
"Everyone is busy."

The man looked around his house, so beautiful with all the party decorations. He was angry, and he felt a little sad, too, because no one wanted to come to the party.

"Go, invite everyone you find in the streets and alleys!" he exclaimed to his servant. "Invite the crippled and blind people who beg in the street."

The servant hurried away. "Come to my master's house," he called to everyone he found in the street.

A blind man held up his bowl, asking for money. "Come to the dinner my master has prepared," the servant said to him.

People looked at the servant curiously as he walked along, calling them to come. They all followed him home.

Inside the big house, the blind man felt his way along the wall leading to the dining room. A crippled man shuffled painfully over the shiny tile floor. All the guests gathered around the table. And still there was room.

"Go outside the city," the master ordered. "Call the people along the roads and out in the fields. Bring thcm in. Not one of those people I invited before will get a taste of my good food!"

The servant hurried to do as his master said. When he returned with those he found, his master's house was filled. And the party began.

When Jesus finished the story, the guests around Nathan's tablc shook their heads. What a strange party! Who would want to invite all those kinds of people to a party?

When Jesus left Nathan's house later that day, He was quickly surrounded by the kinds of people Nathan never invited to dinner: tax collectors and all sorts of poor, lonely and sinful people no one else liked to be with. Jesus loved all of them.

6

JESUS LOVES EVERYONE
Luke 15:1-32

"Look what kind of people come to Jesus!" a Pharisee complained. He stood with his friends watching the tax collectors* and all sorts of sinful and lonely people gather around Jesus.

"Yes," agreed another Pharisee. "Jesus even *welcomes* sinners!"

"He eats with them, too." A scribe shook his head. "Soon He'll be just like them!"

Jesus knew exactly what they were saying. "If you had a hundred sheep," He said, pointing to the first Pharisee, "if one got lost, would you go out to look for it?"

The Pharisee nodded his head, "Yes."

* Tax collectors were hated in Jesus' day because they collected money for the Roman government and often charged people more than was fair.

"Yes," Jesus went on, "you would leave the ninety-nine sheep and search for the lost one. You would look under bushes and climb into ditches just to find it.

"When you found the sheep, you would carry it home and call out to your friends, 'Come, be happy with me because I have found my sheep!'

"There is joy in heaven," Jesus continued, "when one sinner is found who is sorry for his sin. There is much more joy than over the ninety-nine people who think they are good."

The Pharisees and scribes muttered among themselves, but no one dared say anything to Jesus.

"Suppose your wife had ten silver coins," Jesus went on, pointing to a scribe. "If she lost one of them, she wouldn't be satisfied with the other nine. She would clean the house carefully and take a lamp to look into all the dark corners. When she finally found the coin, she would call to all the neighbors, 'Come, be happy with me. I have found my lost coin!'

"In the same way, there is joy in heaven

over one person who is sorry for his sin,"
Jesus said.

Jesus thought for a moment, and then He
began to tell another story. All the people
became quiet so they could hear Jesus. They
liked to listen to His stories.

The story Jesus told them was about a man
who had two sons. The younger son was tired
of living at home. He wanted to go away and
be his own boss and do whatever he pleased.

"Father," the young man said one day,
"give me my share of your property. I want to
enjoy it now while I'm young."

The father knew his son hadn't been happy
for a long time, and he decided to do as his
son asked. The father figured out how much of
his property should go to the young man and
gave him the money for it.

The young man packed up his things. A
few days later he started out on a long journey.
He traveled wherever he wanted and spent all
his time having fun. He never worked.

While the young man was away from
home, his father often stood looking down the

road. "I wonder where my boy is today?" he would say to himself. "God, please keep my son safe," he would pray.

After a while the young man's money was gone. He was in a country where there was very little food. People needed lots of money to buy even a small bit of food. So he decided he should look for a job.

The only job the young man could find was feeding pigs for a farmer. He fed garbage to the pigs. His stomach hurt so much from hunger that he almost wanted to eat some of that garbage himself.

One day he started thinking about how much food there was back at home. Even his father's servants had plenty!

"And here I am starving," he said to himself. He thought about it for a long time. Finally, one morning he got up early and started walking home.

"I know I have no right to be treated like a son," he said to himself as he walked along. "Maybe my father will let me work for him like one of the men he hires to work in the fields." At least he would have food.

The young man walked and walked. He had to stop often and rest because he was so weak and hungry. Finally he got near home.

That very day, the young man's father stood looking down the road again. He was about to go back to work when he saw a tiny figure way off in the distance.

"Who's that?" he asked himself. "Could that be my son coming home?" And as the figure got closer the father shouted, "Yes, that's my boy!" And he took off running down the road to meet his son.

When the young man saw his father running toward him, he began to run to meet him. They ran into each other's arms right there in the middle of the road! The father hugged his son tightly.

"You're back!" he cried, kissing the boy again and again. "You're back!"

The son began to cry too. Then he remembered what he had decided to say to his father, and he pulled away.

"I have done wrong," he said. "I know I

have no right to be called your son any longer.
But . . ."

His father grabbed him, smothering the
words with another hug. He pulled the young
man toward the house and began shouting for
the servants.

"Bring out some decent clothes for this
boy," he ordered. "A ring for his finger and a
pair of good sandals, too," he added.

"Yes, sir," the servant said, hurrying away.

"Kill that calf we've been saving for a celebration," the father called to another servant.
"Let's have a party. My son is back! The lost
one is found!"

The young man bathed and dressed. His
mother brought him some food to eat while
they waited for the calf to roast over the coals.
Musicians were called in to play, and the
servants hurried to invite the neighbors to this
party.

At sunset the older son came in from the
field. He was very tired and hot. How nice it
would be to have a bath and spend a quiet evening by himself!

But when he got near the house he heard the noise and saw the servants hurrying around. "It looks like a party," he said to himself.

Then he grabbed the sleeve of a servant who hurried by. "What's happening?" he asked.

"Your brother came back!" the servant exclaimed. "Your father is giving a party because your brother is safe and well."

"Oh, no!" the young man sat right down where he was. He felt angry and jealous. "That rascal!" he said to himself. "He wouldn't stay home, and he couldn't stay away either."

The father stepped out of the house. "Come in, Son," he said. "Your brother is home!"

"All these years I worked while my brother went away and had fun," the young man complained angrily. "But you never gave me a party. As soon as that rascal comes back after spending all your money doing wrong things, you kill the best calf for a party." The young man was so angry that by this time he was shouting.

The father gave a sad sigh. "Son," he said lovingly, "you're always here. All that is mine is yours. Your brother was as good as dead, but now he's alive. It is right that we should celebrate. He was lost, but now we have him back."

Jesus finished telling the story. He looked around at the crowd. "God cares about the lost, the poor and the sick," He said.

"When someone comes to God and is sorry for his sin, all heaven has a party. It doesn't matter how much wrong the person has done. God is always ready to forgive anyone who is truly sorry."

7

WHEN GOD DOESN'T ANSWER RIGHT AWAY
Luke 17:11-19; 18:1-14;
John 11:1-48

"Jesus!" a voice called out.

Jesus stopped at the village gate and looked around.

"Lepers!"* Peter said sharply, drawing back.

Some men who had leprosy stood together a few feet away. The law said they must stay away from healthy people. They could not live with their families, and they had to beg for food. But they wanted to see Jesus.

"Master!" they called again. "Have mercy on us!" There were ten of them.

* People who have leprosy, a very contagious disease.

Jesus looked at the ten sick men. Some of them leaned on sticks, their feet so deformed that it was hard for them to walk. They watched eagerly as Jesus walked toward them.

The disciples waited by the village gate. They had seen Jesus heal many people, some of them lepers. But they still wondered just what He would do this time.

Jesus stopped in front of the ten men. One at a time, He looked into each of their faces. He felt sad that they suffered so much. They could see on His face how much He cared about them.

"You are healed," Jesus said gently. "Go show yourselves to the priest."

The men stood still, but only for an instant. Then they turned and hobbled away. And as they went, their leprosy disappeared! Jesus had made them well!

Jesus went back to the disciples and they walked into the village together. But they had not gone far when they heard the pounding of someone's feet running behind them in the street.

"Jesus! Jesus!" called a voice. It was one of the lepers!

Jesus stopped and waited. The disciples stepped back. Then they noticed that the man no longer had leprosy.

"Jesus!" the man shouted happily, falling down at Jesus' feet. "Thank you! I'm well! Thank you, Jesus!"

Jesus looked down at the man and smiled. Then He looked toward the gate. "Weren't there ten men healed?" He asked. "Where are the other nine? Has only this Samaritan come back to thank me?"

The man still knelt at Jesus' feet. Jesus looked down at him again. His body was well and strong.

"Get up," Jesus said to the man. "You are healed because you believed in me."

The man got up and hurried away. He was almost dancing, and he kept praising God.

Jesus and the disciples went on to the center of the village and sat down under a tree. People began leaving their homes and gathering around to listen while Jesus taught.

"My Father wants to give you whatever you ask of Him," Jesus said. "But you must learn to keep praying until He answers.

"You should be like the widow* who kept going to a judge about someone who had done wrong to her. The judge didn't love God or care what happened to people. At first he paid no attention to the widow. But she kept going to him anyway.

"At last the judge said to himself, 'I don't care at all about this woman. But she keeps bothering me. I guess I had better do something about her.' And he punished the person who had done wrong to her.

"Though that judge didn't care about God or people, he did what the widow asked because she never gave up," Jesus continued.

"Don't you think God will answer the cries of His children much more quickly than that judge? If He delays you must keep asking."

"God always hears the prayers of good people," said a man in the crowd.

"Yes," added another man. "Some people

* A woman whose husband has died.

disobey God so much that He doesn't listen to them."

Jesus looked at the two men. They seemed so satisfied with themselves that He decided to tell them a story.

"Two men stood in the Temple praying," Jesus began. "One was a Pharisee and the other a tax collector.

"The Pharisee felt very proud of himself. 'God,' he said, 'I'm thankful that I'm not a sinner like other men. I am not greedy or bad.'

"Then he took a peek around to see who might be watching. 'I'm not like that tax collector over there,' he said. 'I fast* two times each week. And I give to God a tithe** of everything I have.'

"But the tax collector stood in a corner alone," Jesus went on. "His head was bowed. 'Oh, God,' he prayed, 'I'm so sinful. Be merciful to me.' "

Jesus paused and looked at the two men for whom He told the story. Then He continued.

---

* To go without food for a long time.
** That's a tenth, like one penny out of every dime.

"The tax collector went home with God's forgiveness," He said. "But the Pharisee needed to learn something before God could forgive him. The Pharisee needed to understand that he was sinful."

The next day Jesus and His disciples continued their journey toward Jerusalem. They traveled slowly, stopping in many villages along the way. In one village a man came running up to them with a message.

"I've been looking all over for you," the man said to Jesus. "Martha and her sister Mary, who live in Bethany, send word that the one whom you love is sick."

"Lazarus is sick?" John asked.

"He is very sick," the man nodded.

"Thank you for bringing me the message," Jesus said. And the man hurried away.

"You can't go to help Lazarus, Lord," Andrew said. "The Pharisees there have already threatened to kill you."

Jesus didn't answer. He was thinking about Mary and Martha and Lazarus. He had often been a guest in their home. Martha liked to make dinner for Him, and Mary and Lazarus always listened to Him carefully.

But now Mary would be sitting beside her brother's bed. Martha would be busy bathing his hot face, tucking in the blankets around him. Perhaps she would be tempting him to eat some of her soup. Jesus smiled, thinking about them.

"This sickness is not to end in death," He finally said quietly. "It is to bring glory to the Son of God."

It was two days later when Jesus finally announced, "Now it's time to go to Bethany."

"But the Pharisees are waiting there to kill you!" Philip reminded Jesus.

"It's still time for me to do my work," Jesus answered. "Lazarus is asleep," He added softly. "I will awaken him."

"He'll be getting better if he's sleeping," John said hopefully.

Jesus looked at John sadly, and John knew he had not understood.

"Lazarus is dead," Jesus said. A sigh of

sadness went up from all the men. "I am glad
I wasn't there," Jesus went on, "so that you
may believe. Come, let's go to Lazarus." And
Jesus began walking toward Bethany.

When Jesus and the disciples got near
Bethany, they saw that the town was filled
with people who had come from Jerusalem to
comfort Martha and Mary. Someone ran to tell
Martha that Jesus was coming, and she hurried
out to meet Him.

"Oh, Lord," Martha cried, falling down on
the road in front of Jesus, "if you had been
here my brother wouldn't have died." The
tears ran down her cheeks, and dropped in the
dust at Jesus' feet.

Jesus looked tenderly down at the sobbing
woman. Finally she raised her head to look up
at Him through the tears which filled her eyes.

"Even now," she said softly, "I know God
will give you anything you ask."

"Your brother will live again," Jesus said,
touching her head gently.

"I know he'll live again in heaven," Martha
answered.

"I am the resurrection and the life," Jesus declared. "Anyone who believes on me will live, even if he has died. And some never will die. Do you believe that, Martha?"

"Oh, yes, Lord," she said. "I know you are the Son of God."

In a few moments Martha got up and hurried home. Jesus watched her go. He knew she would send Mary out to see Him.

Sure enough, a few minutes later Mary came out the village gate. A group of mourners were with her.

Mary fell down at Jesus' feet. "Lord, if you had been here my brother wouldn't have died," she sobbed.

The people who had come out with Mary began to cry loudly.

"Where is Lazarus buried?" Jesus asked, lifting His voice to be heard above the noise.

The mourners stopped crying. "Come and see," they said. One of them took Mary's arm, and they started off toward the tomb.

Soon Jesus stood in front of the cave in which Lazarus had been buried. A big stone

covered the entrance. "Take away the stone,"
He said.

"Oh, Lord," Martha said quickly, "his
body will smell! He died four days ago."

"Didn't I tell you, Martha, that you would
see how wonderful God is if you believe?"
Jesus asked.

Two men put their strong backs to the big
stone. Slowly, they moved the stone until the
entrance was uncovered.

Jesus looked up to heaven. "Father," He
prayed, "I thank you for hearing my prayer. I
know you always hear, but I'm saying it for all
these people to hear. I want them to believe
that you sent me into the world."

Then Jesus turned toward the open cave.
"Lazarus!" He shouted. "Come out!"

The crowd stared at the entrance of the
cave. There was a rustle inside the cave, as if
someone were getting up. The sound grew
louder. In a moment, a white-wrapped form
stumbled out into the sunlight.

"Unwrap him," Jesus said. "Let him go."

Many hands pulled at the folds of cloth

which were wound around Lazarus. Finally he
stood free before them. He shook his head to
loosen the hair matted against his scalp.

Martha and Mary ran to hug their brother.
"Oh, Lazarus!" they exclaimed. "You're alive
again!"

"Praise God! Praise God!" many of the
people cried happily.

But others were silent. They watched with
stony eyes. Before evening they were back in
Jerusalem reporting to the scribes and
Pharisees what had happened.

"Jesus has got to be stopped," the Pharisees
declared angrily, "or the whole country will
end up believing in Him."

8

WHO IS MOST IMPORTANT?
Matthew 19:27-20:16, 20-28

"Jesus," Peter said, "we left everything to follow you." He stopped, thinking about his family at home. He didn't get to see them very often. And then there was his fishing business. The day Jesus had filled his nets with more fish than his boat could hold* he had left his business and never gone fishing again.

Jesus nodded.

"We're still with you," Peter went on. "What will our reward be?"

"God doesn't measure things the way you do," Jesus answered. "You don't get money or things you can own as a reward for serving God.

* Read about it in Luke 5:1-11.

"The kingdom of God* is like a landowner who went to the market early one morning to hire men to work in his field," Jesus explained. "He found some men who agreed to work all day for one denarius.**

"But he still needed more workers. So he went back to the market three times during the day. Each time he found more men, and they agreed to work the rest of the day for a fair wage. The last men were hired just before sunset.

"When sunset came the landowner sent the field foreman*** out with money to pay the workers. Those who were hired last were paid first. They got one denarius for their hour of work.

" 'Oh, I guess we will get more than we thought,' those who were hired first said to one another.

"But when the foreman got to them, he gave them each a denarius, just as they had

---

* When people put God first in their lives.
** A Roman coin, commonly used in those days.
*** The boss.

agreed with the landowner that morning.

" 'That's not fair!' they complained. And they went looking for the landowner. When they found him they said, 'The men who worked only an hour got a denarius. We worked all day, right through the hot afternoon. We should get more.'

" 'Didn't we agree on a wage of one denarius for the day?' the landowner asked. 'Yes,' they answered. 'But . . . '

" 'Then take it and go. I want to pay those who were hired last the same wage I pay you. The money is mine. Are you angry because I'm generous?'

"God measures things differently than do people," Jesus explained. "In the kingdom of God those who serve others will be honored as my Father wishes."

The next morning while the disciples waited for Jesus, the mother of James and John came and called her sons aside. Then the three of them went to Jesus, the mother walking determinedly ahead of the men. She went to Jesus and knelt at His feet.

"Teacher," she said, "I want to ask a favor of you."

"What is it?" Jesus asked.

"When you are king," she said, "I want my sons to sit on either side of you."

"You don't know what you're asking," Jesus answered. Then he turned to the two men. "Can you suffer what I must suffer?" He asked them.

"Oh, yes, we can," they said eagerly.

"You *will* suffer what I must suffer," Jesus said seriously. "But I don't decide who sits on either side of me. My Father in heaven will decide that."

"How could you have asked such a thing?" Peter scolded James and John when their mother was gone.

"Who do you think you are, anyway?" Philip asked, frowning at the brothers.

"Well," James shrugged, "why not us as well as any of the rest of you?"

"Really now!" Andrew exclaimed. And they began to argue about who deserved the place of honor at Jesus' side.

Jesus, sitting nearby, listened. They sounded just like brothers arguing. "Men, listen to me," He finally said.

The disciples stopped arguing and turned to Jesus.

"Those who are kings or rulers on earth boss others around. The more people they can boss around, the more important you think they are.

"But that is not God's way, nor mine. It isn't to be that way with you, either." Then He turned to look at James and John. "If you want to be important," He said, "you must serve others. Anyone who wants to be boss must become like a servant to others."

John shook his head. *That doesn't make sense,* he thought.

Servants get bossed around all the time, James thought. Then he said, "I do not see anything very important about that."

"The Son of man came to give up His life for many," Jesus said solemnly. "And that is the example you should follow. You must give up your life to care for people."

9

A CHEATER, A BLIND MAN AND SOME PERFUME
Luke 19:1-10; Mark 10:46-52;
John 12:1-8

Zacchaeus the tax collector looked around
his stall in the Jericho market. It was the
biggest stall any tax collector had, and he felt
very proud. He was the chief tax collector, and
he was very rich.

Some children ran quickly past Zacchaeus's
stall. "Jesus is coming! Jesus is coming!" they
shouted to one another eagerly.

"Jesus?" Zacchaeus asked, leaning out of
his stall to see what was happening in the
street. "Oh, I want to see Jesus!" He looked at
his work, spread out on the table. "I think I'll

take the day off," he decided. And he put his things away and closed the stall securely.

The market square was already crowded. Zacchaeus pushed and wiggled his way between people. But wherever he turned, all he could see was people towering above him.

Zacchaeus had a problem! He was so short that even some of the children could see more than he could, because they rode on their fathers' shoulders or watched from their mothers' arms.

Zacchaeus almost felt like crying. How could he ever see Jesus in this crowd! And then he had an idea!

"I'll climb a tree!" he said.

A man beside him turned to look down at him strangely. But Zacchaeus paid no attention. He was already pushing his way through the crowd toward a big sycamore tree at the opposite end of the square. Finally he stood at the base of the huge, spreading tree. It looked like a long way up to the first limb.

Zacchaeus took a deep breath and began to climb the tree. He hadn't climbed a tree in a long time, and it was harder than he remembered. But he finally reached one of the thick strong limbs which grew out over the square. He sat on the limb and leaned back against the trunk of the tree. He looked down.

There was Jesus! He was moving slowly through the square, talking with the people around Him. The crowd pressed in from every side.

Zacchaeus thought, *Huh! He doesn't look so special!* But he kept his eyes on Jesus just the same.

Jesus finally walked into the shade of the sycamore. He walked by the thick old trunk and stopped right under the branch on which Zacchaeus sat. Then Jesus looked up.

Zacchaeus caught his breath. If everyone looked at him they might laugh. A grown man in a tree! Not very dignified!

Jesus looked right at Zacchaeus. But He didn't laugh. He just smiled and said, "Come on down, Zacchaeus. I'd like to go to your house."

Suddenly Zacchaeus forgot all about how

he looked. Quickly he slid down the tree to the ground, catching his coat on knobby spots on the trunk. But he was too excited to care.

Proudly Zacchaeus led Jesus to his house.

"We have a guest!" he shouted to his servants when he and Jesus entered the courtyard. "Cook up a special dinner."

While the servants prepared a delicious meal, Jesus and Zacchaeus had a very serious talk. After dinner, Zacchaeus stood in front of his family and the servants to tell Jesus what he had decided.

"I have done wrong by taking money that did not belong to me," he said. "I'm very sorry for my sin, and I'm going to give half my riches to the poor.

"And to those people I have cheated," he went on, "I will repay four times what I took from them."

"Today you have believed in the Lord, Zacchaeus," Jesus said, smiling. "The Son of man came to earth to find and save people like you."

The next morning when Jesus got ready to

leave Jericho, a huge crowd gathered around Him and followed Him out of the city. Outside the city gate, Jesus heard someone shouting.

"Jesus, Son of David, have mercy on me!" a man called.

"Hush!" the people around the man said. "Jesus is busy with more important things than bothering with you!"

But the man cried out even louder. "Jesus! Son of David, have mercy on me!"

Jesus stopped. "What is it?" He asked. "Who is calling out?"

"Oh, just a blind beggar, Rabbi," a man near the edge of the crowd answered.

"Bring him here," Jesus ordered.

The people who had been telling the beggar to be quiet helped him up and led him to Jesus.

"What do you want me to do?" Jesus asked when the beggar stood in front of Him.

"Oh, Rabbi," the blind man pleaded, "I want to see!"

How sad, Jesus thought. *This man has never seen the sunshine or the flowers!* Jesus knew how very much the man wanted to see.

"You are healed," Jesus said, reaching out and touching the man's eyes gently.

Immediately the man began to look around, blinking a little in the bright sunlight. Everything looked so beautiful!

"Oh, thank you, Jesus!" he cried. Then he ran back to the gate and picked up his coat. And he followed Jesus.

That day, Jesus traveled on to Bethany with His disciples. In Bethany, they went as usual to the home of their friends, Mary, Martha and Lazarus.

While they were in Bethany, a man named Simon invited them to his house for dinner. Lazarus was also invited, and Martha helped serve the dinner.

Mary went to Simon's house, too. But she stood in the shadows watching while the men ate and talked. She put her hand into the folds of her skirt to feel for the flask of perfume she had hidden there. She had bought the perfume with some silver coins she had saved for a long time. She wanted to use the perfume to show Jesus how much she loved Him.

The men were too busy with good food and their talk to notice when Mary slipped quietly to the foot of Jesus' divan. She knelt down and pulled the flask from its hiding place. She broke the seal, pouring the perfume over Jesus' feet.

Immediately the lovely smell filled the house. Martha stopped to watch as she held a large platter of food. The men around the table sat up tall, trying to see what was happening.

"Mary," someone asked sharply, "why did you do that?"

But Mary paid no attention. Gently she wiped Jesus' feet with her long hair.

"What a waste!" someone exclaimed.

"Yes," said Judas Iscariot, one of the disciples. "That perfume could have been sold for lots of money. And the money could have been given to the poor." His eyes glinted greedily as he reached down to touch the leather money pouch he always carried on his belt.

"Let her alone!" Jesus said sharply. Then

He looked at Mary. "She has anointed me ahead of time for my burial. There will always be poor people to help, but I won't be with you much longer."

Anointed for His burial? What could Jesus mean? The disciples thought He must be talking in riddles.

10

A PARADE
FOR THE KING
Luke 19:28-44; Mark 11:11; 12:41-44;
Matthew 25:14-30

Peter and John walked into the village.
There, right in front of them, stood a colt tied
up near a house.

"Just like Jesus said!" John exclaimed as he
walked over to the colt and began to untie it.

"Wait!" called one of the men who stood
nearby. "Why are you untying my colt?"

"The Lord needs it," Peter answered just as
Jesus had told him to.

"Oh, all right," the man said. "I would be
honored to let the Lord use my colt."

"We'll bring the colt back later," John
added as he and Peter walked away leading the
animal.

When Peter and John took the colt to Jesus, He said, "I'm going into Jerusalem."

"Jesus will enter Jerusalem like a king!" the disciples began to exclaim excitedly. They spread their coats on the colt's back for Jesus to sit on.

Jesus got on the colt and began to ride down the road toward Jerusalem. The disciples followed along. The crowds that were going to Jerusalem for the Passover* recognized Jesus at once.

"The King is coming!" they cried joyfully.

"Hosanna** to the Son of David!"

The disciples and some of the people spread their coats on the road ahead of the colt to make a carpet. Others pulled branches from the palm trees along the way and put them on the road.

The crowd grew bigger and bigger as more people joined the parade. They waved palm branches and shouted their joy.

* Yearly celebration remembering the time the children of Israel escaped from Egypt.
** A Hebrew word meaning "Save us," which was used to praise the power of a great leader.

"Blessed is the King of Israel!"

"Blessed is the one who comes in God's name!"

The disciples walked along shouting happily with the crowd.

Jesus will soon be our king! Andrew thought as he shouted, "Hosanna!"

When they got near the city gate, John looked over at Jesus. He let his arm fall to his side, the palm branch dragging in the dust. Jesus was crying!

"Oh, Jerusalem!" Jesus sobbed.

How Jesus loved Jerusalem! How He loved the Temple!

"Oh, Jerusalem," Jesus cried, "if only you knew who could give you peace! You will be destroyed because you didn't know when God visited you."

John walked the rest of the way in silence. No one else seemed to notice Jesus' tears. They shouted their joy all the way to the Temple.

At the Temple, Jesus got off the colt and went into the outer court. It was filled with noisy, sweating people who had come to the Passover. And caged animals waiting to be offered to God were everywhere.

Some of the people who had been in the parade followed Jesus through the court, still singing their praises. But they dropped their palm branches in surprise when Jesus began turning over the money changers' tables and chased out everyone who was buying and selling. "It is written in Scriptures," Jesus said, " 'My house is a place for prayer, not a thieves' den.' "

The next morning Jesus went back to the Temple.

People soon crowded around Jesus, still expecting Him to take over the country and become their king. During the next few days He taught them about the kingdom of God and told them what would happen at the end of time.

One day when Jesus had finished teaching, He sat down near the money chests where people put their gifts for God. He watched as they walked by the chests and dropped their money inside.

A Pharisee walked up carrying a bulging
leather purse. He opened it and turned it
upside down, letting the gold coins clink
noisily into the chest. He glanced around,
hoping people had noticed how many coins he
gave.

A very rich man, followed by a servant,
walked up to the chest. He took his purse from
the servant, counted out a large handful of
coins, and dropped them, one by one, into the
money chest. He also wanted everyone to
know that he was giving lots of money.

Later a widow came, carrying a small child
and leading a little boy.* She looked very
tired. Her clothes were worn and the boy's
tunic had been carefully mended many times.

"Put the coins in, Josiah," the woman said
quietly. "This is our offering to God."

The little boy stood on tiptoe so he could
see. He dropped two small copper coins into
the chest.

"Did you see that?" Jesus asked His
disciples.

* The Bible does not say the widow had children. We're
imagining that she did.

"She had so little to give," John said. "Poor woman."

"She gave more than anyone else," Jesus said. "She gave all she had. The others have so much they will hardly miss what they gave."

Later Jesus told His disciples a story about how God wants people to use their money, and everything else they have, to serve Him. He said the kingdom of God was like a man who planned a long journey. Before he left he gave three of his servants some money.

The master gave the first servant $5,000. The second servant he gave $2,000, and the third $1,000.

"Use this money until I return," the master said. And then he left.

The first servant carefully planned how to use the money. He bought an olive orchard. When the olives ripened, he made oil from them and sold it.*

He kept doing that each time the olives were harvested. Finally he had earned $10,000.

* The Bible does not tell us how the servants used the money.

The second servant bought a stall in the market where he could have a store. He worked very hard, buying and selling things. And soon he had earned $4,000.

The third servant couldn't decide how to use his money. It didn't seem like much, and he was afraid he would lose it. So one night he sneaked out of the village, dug a hole in the ground and put his coins in the hole. Then he filled the hole with dirt and covered the spot with leaves and twigs so no one would see it.

After a very long time, the master came back. He called his servants to see what they had done with the money while he was gone.

When the first servant brought him $10,000, the master was very happy. "You have done a good job!" he exclaimed. "I will give you more of my property to look after."

The second servant gave the master the $4,000 he had earned. "Good!" said the master. "I will put you in charge of more of my things."

Finally the third servant came, carrying the same coins his master had given him. "I know

you are a hard man to please," the servant
said. "So I hid your money to keep it safe.
And here it all is."

"What!" shouted the master. "You could at
least have put my money in a savings account
so it would earn interest!" He turned to a
servant who stood nearby. "Take his $1,000,"
he said, "and give it to the man who earned
$10,000. He'll know how to use it. And throw
this lazy servant out!"

After Jesus finished the story, He said to
His disciples, "God has given you all you
have. And He expects you to make use of
whatever He has given you.

. "If you have money, you must use it in a
way that shows love for God. Or if you have a
talent, something you can do especially well,
you must also use that in a way that shows
you love Him."

The disciples listened carefully. They
thought for a long time about what Jesus said.
Later, when Jesus had gone back to heaven,
they learned to do as Jesus had taught them.

11

A FAREWELL DINNER
Matthew 26:17-30, 36-47;
John 13:1-30

Jesus and His disciples climbed the steps to the large upstairs room. Peter and John had been there all day, preparing for the Passover meal.

"This is a good place!" Andrew said. "Just right for us."

"We found this room by following a man who carried a water jar," Peter smiled.

"Just like Jesus told us!" John said.

Jesus smiled and motioned for the men to sit down. They gathered around the long table, and the celebration of the Passover began.

"I have been so eager to eat this Passover meal with you," Jesus said while they ate.

"This will be my last Passover until the Lamb of God* has died for all."

The last Passover? What did Jesus mean? The disciples wondered. But they silently ate the bitter herbs, unleavened bread** and roast lamb which reminded them of the escape of their people from Egypt hundreds of years before.

When the dinner was nearly over, Jesus got up from the table and took off His coat. He tied a big towel around His waist. Then He picked up a basin from the floor and poured clean water into it. The disciples watched curiously, wondering what He was going to do.

Jesus carried the basin of water to the foot of Andrew's divan and set it on the floor. "Put your feet in the water," He said. Then He washed Andrew's feet and dried them with the towel He had tied around His waist.

Next Jesus washed Thomas's feet. Then Judas Iscariot's and John's. The disciples

* A name for Jesus. See dictionary.
** Bread without yeast or anything else to make it light and soft.

watched silently. They wondered why Jesus was washing everyone's feet. It was a job for servants, not for Jesus!

When Jesus set the basin down at the foot of Peter's divan, Peter asked what they all wanted to know. "Lord, why should you wash my feet?"

"You don't understand now, Peter," Jesus answered. "But you will later."

"Jesus, you are not a servant," Peter declared, pulling his feet up on the divan. "You shouldn't wash my feet."

"If I don't wash your feet," Jesus said, "you don't belong with me."

"Oh, I belong with you!" Peter exclaimed. "You can wash my head and my hands, too." And he reached impulsively toward the basin.

"Only your feet," Jesus said.

Jesus continued around the circle until He had washed the feet of all the disciples. Then He put the basin and towel aside. He put on His coat again and took His place at the table.

"Do you know what I've done?" He asked. "You call me Teacher and Lord, and you are

right. But I have washed your feet like a
servant. If I, your Teacher, can serve you, you
must serve one another."

The disciples were quiet, thinking about
what Jesus said. They remembered His telling
them before that the one who wanted to be
most important should serve the others. But
they still could not understand it. Soon they
forgot about it and began to talk among
themselves.

While the disciples talked, Jesus was silent.
He was thinking about serious things. His face
was sad. "Let me tell you something," He
finally said.

The men stopped talking in mid-sentence
and turned to look at Jesus.

"One of you will give me to my enemies,"
Jesus said sadly.

"What? Never!" the disciples exclaimed.

"Who would do that?"

"Lord, would I ever do that?"

They began to look at one another
suspiciously. Which of them could possibly do
such a terrible thing?

"Is it I?" Judas Iscariot finally asked. There was a hard glint in his eyes.

"You have said it," Jesus answered. Then He added, "Do quickly what you're going to do."

Judas got up and hurried from the room. It was a strange time to leave the Passover meal, but none of the other disciples thought much about it. Judas carried the money for all of them. Perhaps Jesus wanted him to buy supplies for the remaining days of the Passover.

Jesus turned to the plate of unleavened bread on the table. He picked up a piece, held it in His hands and thanked God for it. Then He broke it in pieces and passed it to the disciples.

"Eat this," He said. "This represents my body which is given for you."

Next He held a cup of wine between His hands and again thanked God. "Drink this," He said, passing the cup to each of the disciples. "This represents my blood which I will shed to save the world from sin."

After everyone had taken a sip of wine
Jesus held the cup again in His hand. "This is
the last time I will drink wine until we are
together in my Father's kingdom," He said
quietly.

His Father's kingdom? The disciples
wondered just what Jesus was talking about.
There were so many questions they wanted to
ask Him.

Jesus knew their questions. He had many
things to say to them, to prepare them for what
would soon happen. He talked to them for a
long time. Finally He prayed for them.

When Jesus and His disciples left the
upstairs room much later, the whole city
seemed to be asleep. They walked silently
through the streets of Jerusalem to the Mount
of Olives.

"You wait here while I pray," Jesus said,
stopping under some trees in Gethsemane
Garden. The disciples sat down on the ground.

"Come," Jesus said softly, turning to Peter,
James and John. And as they had done so

often before, the three men followed Jesus away from the group.

"I am filled with sadness," Jesus said in a low voice. "Please stay here and pray with me."

"Yes, Lord," Peter said firmly. "We will pray."

Jesus went a few feet away and knelt to pray, bending forward until His forehead touched the ground.

"Please, Father," He cried, "if it's possible, don't let this terrible thing happen to me. But I do want your will to be done."

Finally He straightened up. He wanted so much to know that His friends were praying with Him. He got up and walked over to the three disciples.

"Peter!" He said, as He touched Peter's shoulder. "Are you sleeping?"

Peter sat up and rubbed his eyes. James and John stirred.

"You couldn't even pray with me one hour?" Jesus asked sadly. "Stay awake and pray!"

Jesus left the disciples again, and they tried to stay awake. But their eyes were so heavy! The next thing they knew Jesus was waking them again.

John groaned as he looked into Jesus' perspiring face. He loved Jesus, and he really wanted to stay awake and pray with Him. But before long, the three disciples were all asleep again.

Jesus came back a third time. "Still asleep?" He asked. "Never mind. It's too late now."

Suddenly the three men came wide awake. Soldiers were coming toward them, their armor clanking. A crowd of people followed. Their faces seemed to dance strangely by the flickering light of the torches they carried in their hands.

"Soldiers!" John exclaimed.

"And Temple guards," James added.

"Oh, no!" Peter groaned. For there, in front of the crowd, was Judas Iscariot leading the way.

12

THE KING'S TRIAL
Matthew 26:47—27:30; Luke
22:47—23:24; John 18:1—19:16

The mob of soldiers and Temple guards
rushed toward Jesus, swords and clubs ready in
their hands. Calmly He walked toward them
instead of trying to run away as they expected
Him to.

"Master!" Judas Iscariot exclaimed,
stepping forward to kiss Jesus on the cheek.
Then he stepped back. His job was finished.

The soldiers grabbed Jesus roughly and tied
His hands tightly behind His back. Then
shouting and waving their swords, they
dragged Him away to the house of Caiaphas,*
the high priest. The chief priests and scribes

* KI-ah-fuss. Leader of all the priests.

were waiting there to find a way to have Jesus put to death.

The disciples ran away. Some watched from the shadows. They were so frightened that they hardly dared to breathe. After a few minutes Peter and John followed the mob to Caiaphas's house. When they arrived, Jesus was already inside.

John walked up to the gate outside Caiaphas's house and spoke to the gatekeeper. She knew him, so she opened the gate. He went into the courtyard and stood near the fire with soldiers, Temple guards and servants from Caiaphas's household. When John glanced back at the gate, he saw Peter standing outside.

John went to the gatekeeper. "That man is a friend of mine," he said. "Please let him in."

John returned to his place by the fire, and the girl swung open the big gate. "Aren't you one of Jesus' disciples?" she asked, looking at Peter curiously.

"Oh, no," Peter said quickly. "I don't know Him."

Peter went to stand in the shadows near the fire. Soon he stepped up to warm his icy hands by the hot coals.

"Why, you're one of the Galilean's disciples!" a guard exclaimed, looking at Peter. "I saw you in the garden with Him."

"I don't know what you're talking about," Peter declared, a chill of fear running up his spine. He turned his back to the fire, hoping no one else would notice him.

Time dragged by slowly. Peter and John waited anxiously, wondering what was happening to Jesus inside the house. Somewhere nearby a rooster crowed. Soon it would be dawn.

The door to Caiaphas's house finally burst open. Soldiers and guards surged down the stairs, dragging Jesus behind them. Peter and John turned to watch.

"You are one of His disciples," said a voice beside Peter. Peter turned to look at the servant who stared at him. "You even have a Galilean accent," the servant added.

"No, sir!" Peter exclaimed.

Just then the rooster crowed again, and Peter remembered what Jesus had said earlier. "By the time the rooster crows twice, Peter, you will say three times that you don't know me."

Peter caught his breath and glanced at Jesus. Jesus was looking sadly at him. Peter turned away from Jesus' gaze and ran quickly out the gate. Outside he sank into a dark corner and began to cry. He sat there crying for a long time before he got up to see where Jesus had been taken.

Soldiers and guards, followed by the chief priests and scribes, took Jesus to the judgment hall to be tried by Pilate, the Roman governor. The Jews were not allowed to put anyone to death, so they planned to convince Pilate to do it for them.

Strict Jewish laws kept the priests and scribes from entering the judgment hall during the Passover. So they stood outside and Pilate walked out to hear their charges against Jesus.

"This man calls Himself the Messiah!" the Jewish leaders cried.

Pilate went inside the judgment hall where Jesus waited with the soldiers. "Are you the King of the Jews?" he asked.

"Yes, it is as you say," Jesus answered quietly. "Why do you ask?"

"I don't know anything about Jewish law," Pilate said. "Your own people brought you here."

"My kingdom is not an earthly one," Jesus said. "If it were, my friends would defend me."

"Then you really are a king?" Pilate asked.

"I am the King," Jesus answered. "That is why I came into the world."

Pilate returned to the mob outside, shaking his head. "This man is not guilty of any crime," he declared.

"He stirs up people against Caesar,"* they cried. "He did it in Galilee, and He's doing it here."

"Is He from Galilee?" Pilate asked. "Take Him to Herod. Herod rules Galilee."

Pilate walked back inside and firmly closed

* The head of all the Roman Empire.

the big double doors. The soldiers took Jesus
outside and headed toward Herod's palace.

Herod was very excited when he heard that
Jesus was coming. "Show me a miracle!" he
exclaimed when Jesus stood before him.

But Jesus did not say a word.

"Can't you talk?" Herod demanded.

The chief priests and scribes kept shouting
their charges against Jesus, but Herod paid
little attention to them. He asked Jesus many
questions, but Jesus did not answer.

Finally Herod told his soldiers to put a
royal robe on Jesus. Then they began to make
fun of Him by bowing to Him. When they
tired of their game, Herod directed the soldiers
to take Jesus back to Pilate.

As Pilate heard the mob returning, he
sighed heavily. He thought maybe Jesus really
was a god, and he was afraid to have Jesus
killed. But the Jewish people were so upset
that Pilate knew he must do more than let
Jesus go.

Then Pilate had an idea. Barabbas!
Everyone hated Barabbas the thief. Surely the

people would not want Barabbas set free!
Pilate could offer to trade Jesus for Barabbas.

Pleased with his idea, Pilate stood up and
went outside to the mob. "Every year at
Passover," he said, "I release a prisoner. This
year you may choose. I will free Barabbas, the
robber. Or I'll release Jesus, the Messiah."

"Release Barabbas!" the crowd roared.
"Crucify Jesus!"

"But Jesus has done no wrong," Pilate said
sadly.

"Crucify Him! Crucify Him!"

Pilate sat down and called for Jesus.
Roughly the soldiers pushed Jesus ahead of
them. He staggered forward through the big
double doors of the judgment hall. Blood had
dried in streaks on His face. His body was
bruised from the beatings He had been given.

"Look at your King!" Pilate shouted.

"Away with Him!" the mob cried. "Crucify
Him!"

"Shall I crucify your King?" Pilate asked.

"Caesar is our king," they answered.
"Crucify Jesus! Crucify Jesus!"

Then Pilate called for a basin of water. He washed his hands carefully. "I wash my hands of this," he said. "I am not responsible for killing a good man."

"We'll take the blame," the chief priests answered.

Then Pilate gave orders to have Barabbas released, and he told the Roman soldiers to crucify Jesus.

The soldiers immediately called out their whole battalion.* Spurred on by one another's laughter, they clothed Jesus in purple and red robes. Quickly they wove together some thorny branches from a bush which grew outside the judgment hall. They formed it into a crown and pressed it on Jesus' head. Blood from the sharp thorns began to flow down His face and neck.

"Here's your sceptre, O King," they laughed, pressing a stick into Jesus' hand.

"Hail, King of the Jews!" they shouted, bowing to make fun of Jesus.

One of the soldiers grabbed the stick from

* A large group of soldiers who work together.

Jesus' hand and began hitting Him with it. One after another, they took turns beating Him. All the while, they kept chanting, "Hail, King of the Jews."

Jesus stood with His head bowed. The soldiers began to circle Him, spitting in His face. He closed His eyes and mouth against their spit. He knew it was all a part of what had to happen before God's plan to save the world would be completed.

13

THE DEATH
OF THE KING

Matt. 27:31-44; Luke 23:32-46;
John 19:25-30,38-42

Jesus staggered along, carrying the heavy
wooden beams of the cross upon which He
would die. Soldiers followed Him, flicking
their whips whenever He slowed down or
stumbled.

Perspiration soaked Jesus' clothes and ran
down His face. He was very weak from the
soldiers' beatings. But He forced Himself to
place one foot in front of the other and walk
on. At last He crumpled under the load. He lay
on the street, pinned under the heavy wooden
beams of the cross.

"Here!" barked a soldier, grabbing a big

man named Simon from the crowd following
Jesus. "You carry this."

Before Simon could say a word, he found
the rough wooden beams being heaved to his
shoulders. It was a heavy load, even for such a
strong man. But he managed to carry it all the
way to Golgotha, the place outside the city
where people were crucified.

At Golgotha the soldiers quickly fastened
together the wooden beams to make a cross.
Then they stripped Jesus of His coat and tunic
and made Him lie down on the cross.

They pounded huge spikes into Jesus'
hands and feet. Then the cross was lifted and
dropped with a dull thud into a hole in the
ground.

On either side of Jesus, the soldiers raised
the crosses of two thieves. Then they settled
down to watch until the three men died.

"Oh, Father," Jesus breathed, looking
down at the soldiers. "Oh, Father, forgive
them. They don't know what they are doing."

People walked along the road nearby,
entering or leaving Jerusalem. "Look at Him!"

they laughed, pointing at Jesus. "He saved other people, but He can't save Himself."

"If you are the Messiah," one of the thieves called to Jesus, "save us and yourself, too!"

"Hush!" warned the other thief. "We are being punished for our sins. But Jesus never did anything wrong." Then he turned to Jesus. "Remember me in your kingdom," he begged.

"You'll be with me in heaven today," Jesus answered.

Blood flowed freely from the wounds in Jesus' hands and feet. His head throbbed with pain from the crown of thorns the soldiers had earlier pressed on His head. His body hurt so much that breathing was hard.

Even with all the pain, He noticed that some of His friends and followers stood nearby. Mary, His mother, was among them. She was sobbing so hard, her whole body shook. She felt sad, alone and helpless. She could not quiet her sobs.

Jesus looked down. He wanted so much to comfort His mother. "Woman," He said.

Mary looked up at Jesus through her tears. She tried to stop sobbing so she could hear Him.

"See your son," Jesus said gently.

Mary turned to look at John, Jesus' disciple, standing nearby.

"John," Jesus continued, "see your mother."

John looked over at the mother of Jesus. He stepped to her side and put his arm around her shoulders.

Mary felt the comfort of her Son's special friend, and her sobs quieted to soft weeping.

The soldiers waited, and Jesus' friends watched. Slowly, very slowly, the hours went by. Then suddenly at noon the sky began to darken. The shadow of the earth moved across the sun until the sun could not be seen. It was like evening in the middle of the day!

"Oh, God," Jesus cried suddenly, gathering all His strength. "Oh, God, why have you left me alone?"

The people around the cross turned to look at Jesus.

"It is done," Jesus said. His head fell forward until His chin rested on His chest. "Father, I put myself in your hands," He cried hoarsely. And then He breathed no more.

Late that afternoon a Jewish leader named Joseph went to Pilate. He asked for the body of Jesus and carried it to his house.

Nicodemus, the Pharisee who had once visited Jesus at night, brought some spices. Together the two men wrapped Jesus' body, along with the spices, in long strips of cloth. Then they placed His body lovingly in a new cave in Joseph's garden. They covered the cave opening with a big rock.

After that the men hurried home, for the Sabbath had come.

14

A HAPPY ENDING
Mark 16:1-8; Luke 24:44-53;
John 20:1-30

It was a sad and lonely Sabbath. Jesus'
disciples and some of His other friends spent
the day together in the upstairs room where
they had celebrated the Passover with Jesus a
few days earlier.

At sunset when the Sabbath was over,
some of the women who loved Jesus prepared
spices to put on His body. Very early the next
morning they walked quietly to Jesus' tomb in
Joseph's garden.

"How will we get the big rock away from
the cave opening?" they wondered as they
walked along.

"Look!" Mary Magdalene exclaimed when

they entered the garden. "The rock has already been moved!"Mary ran to tell Peter and John. The other women cautiously moved forward and stooped to look inside the cave.

Then they got the fright of their lives. A young man clothed from head to foot in white was sitting inside the cave.

"Don't be afraid," the young man said. "Jesus isn't here. See where He lay?" and he pointed to the place where Jesus' body had been. "Go, tell the disciples that Jesus will see them in Galilee."

As soon as the young man stopped talking, the women turned and ran quickly out of the cave and away from the garden.

Meanwhile, Mary Magdalene found Peter and John. "He's gone!" she cried. "Jesus' body is gone."

Peter and John looked at each other. Then without a word they jumped up and ran toward Joseph's garden.

John ran ahead. When he came to the cave, he stooped to look inside. He was still looking when Peter came puffing up and ran right past him into the cave. John followed more slowly.

The two men looked silently at the empty shroud.* The head cloth was neatly folded, lying right where Jesus' head had been. They finally turned and walked away in silence.

Mary Magdalene walked slowly back to the garden, thinking about who might have stolen the body of Jesus. After Peter and John left the garden, she stood outside the cave crying. She stooped to look inside again and caught her breath. Two angels were sitting inside right where the body of Jesus had been.

"Why are you crying?" the angels asked her.

"Because they took away my Lord's body and I don't know where it is," she sobbed. She turned away.

"Why are you crying?" asked another voice.

Mary Magdalene looked up through her tears. "Oh, sir," she cried, thinking she was speaking to the gardener, "where did you take Him?"

* The cloth which had been wrapped around Jesus' body.

"Mary," the man spoke quietly.

Mary gasped. There was no mistaking that voice! She brushed the tears from her eyes and looked up, right into the loving eyes of the Lord Jesus.

"Teacher!" she exclaimed joyfully.

A few minutes later Mary Magdalene left the garden and ran quickly through the streets to the upstairs room. "He's alive!" she cried to the disciples as she burst into the room. "Jesus is alive!"

The men looked at one another, shaking their heads.

"He talked to me," Mary Magdalene insisted. And she told them exactly what had happened.

"Poor woman," the men shook their heads. "She is crazy with sadness."

But that evening when the disciples, all except Thomas, were together, they heard a familiar voice.

"Peace to you," said the voice.

The disciples turned quickly, their eyes wide. There stood Jesus, smiling at them.

For a moment the disciples were silent. Then Jesus held up His hands with the imprints of the nails still showing.

"See my hands," He said. "And my feet." He lifted a sandaled foot.

"Oh, Jesus!" they cried. Sounds of praise soon filled the room.

"We're so glad to see you, Lord!"

After Jesus had talked with them for a while, He said, "Peace to you. As my Father sent me, I will send you."

And then He was gone.

Thomas walked into the room a few minutes later.

"We saw Jesus!" the other disciples exclaimed.

Thomas looked around at them. "How can I believe that?" he asked. "Jesus is dead!"

"But He did come!" Andrew insisted. He stood right where you're standing now."

Thomas shook his head. "I'll believe it when I can put my finger in the wounds in Jesus' hands and feet."

A week later Thomas had a chance to do

just that. Jesus appeared in the room again, just as He had before.

"Peace to you," He said. Then He looked at Thomas. "Come here," He said gently. "Put your finger in the nail prints in my hands and feet."

Thomas looked at Jesus with wide eyes, and he *knew* it was Jesus. "My Lord," he cried, falling down at Jesus' feet. "My God!"

During the next few weeks, Jesus appeared to His followers many times. Once He met several of them in Galilee.

Another time He had breakfast ready on the beach when Peter and his friends had finished a night of fishing.

One day He came to them again when they were all together in the upstairs room.

"I want you to go into the whole world, telling everyone about me," He said to them. "Everything has happened just as the prophets* said it would. The Messiah had to suffer and

* Men in the Old Testament who told how the Messiah would be born, live and die.

die and rise from the dead the third day.

"Now you who were with me and saw it all," He went on, "you must tell the whole world."

Then Jesus led the disciples out of Jerusalem, along the familiar streets and paths to the Mount of Olives. There on top of the mount He stood tall against the sky and lifted His hands to bless them. While He spoke, a cloud surrounded Him and took Him up out of their sight.

Jesus had returned to His Father, God, in heaven. The disciples looked at one another. Then slowly they walked back to Jerusalem, but they were not sad. They knew Jesus was with them. Before long they began preaching on the streets and in the Temple.

"Jesus lives!" they said. "Jesus died to take the punishment for our sin. And now He lives forever!"

Jesus had gone to heaven, but it was not the end. It was really the beginning, the beginning of His kingdom.

DICTIONARY

denarius. A silver coin used by the Romans. In Bible times if a man worked all day he earned one denarius.

hosanna. A Hebrew expression meaning "save us," which was used to praise the power of a great leader.

Lamb of God. A name given to Jesus to tell us more about Him. Just as a man brought a lamb to the altar to make things right with God because the man had sinned (Leviticus 4:32-35), so God gave His "Lamb" (the Lord Jesus) to die for our sins (John 1:29).

lawyer. An expert in understanding the law, a scribe. See SCRIBE for more information.

Levite. A Jewish man of the tribe of Levi, 25 to 50 years of age. These men were set apart to serve in the Tabernacle or in the Temple.

Passover. One of the most important of the Jewish festivals. On this day Jews were instructed to kill a lamb and then roast it. On the first Passover in Egypt the people sprinkled blood on the doorposts so that the Angel of Death would *pass over* their houses.

Pharisee. A Jew in the time of Jesus who tried very hard to obey every part of the law. At first they sincerely tried to please God and to be holy, but later most of them just worried about keeping every little rule. Jesus scolded them because often they were phonies. On the outside they seemed very holy, but inside they were full of lies and hate (Matthew 23).

priest. Among the Jews, a man who served God, offering sacrifices in the Tabernacle and later in the Temple.

Samaritans. The people of Samaria in New Testament times. The Jews wanted to have nothing to do with the Samaritans because they were only half-Jews. Their religion was the worship of the true God, mixed with strange words and doings. Jesus showed that He loved the Samaritans as much as any other people.

Sanhedrin. The group of Jewish leaders in New Testament times chosen to do the work of judges, both in everyday matters and religious questions. The Sanhedrin was made up of the high priest and 70 other members. They were all men, and all true Jews. The Sanhedrin had police at its command, but they could not put a lawbreaker to death. Such cases they had to take to the Romans. Jesus was tried before the Sanhedrin.

scribe. An expert in understanding the law, a lawyer. Most of the scribes in New Testament times were Pharisees who studied and taught the law (Matthew 2:4). Most of the scribes did not like Jesus' teachings.

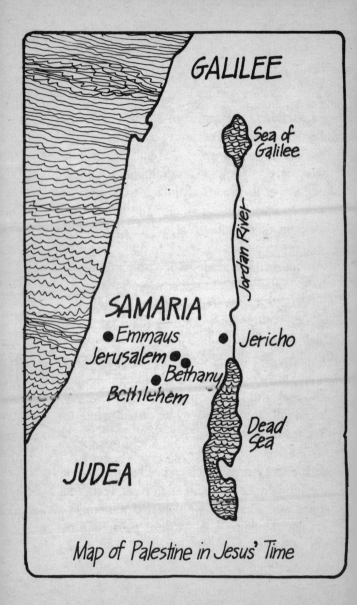

Map of Palestine in Jesus' Time

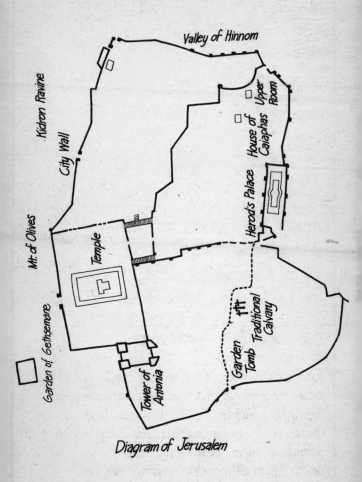

Valley of Hinnom

Kidron Ravine

City Wall

Mt. of Olives

Garden of Gethsemane

Upper Room

House of Caiaphas

Herod's Palace

Garden Tomb

Traditional Calvary

Temple

Tower of Antonia

Diagram of Jerusalem

About the Author

Alice Schrage began her writing career in 1974
after spending ten years on the mission field in
Brazil. She and her husband, Roger, lead
church seminars on spiritual gifts. Mrs.
Schrage is currently involved in the
development of a peer counseling program.
The Schrages have two daughters.